# "Can I Xerox That for You?"

A Professional Reseller's Guide to Understanding
Managed Print Services

~~~~~~~~~~~~~~~~~~~~~~~~~~~~~~~~~~~~~~~~~~~

## By Paige Coverage

Special Advisor to Xerox CEO Ursula Burns, 2008-2011

Begin!

ETL Industrial Publications

Published by Electric Loser Land
51 Sixth Street, San Francisco, California 94103
$\mathcal{ELL}$ 2018
ISBN **13:** 978-1508909514

The following columns appeared originally March 2008 to March 2011 as the centerpiece language for Xerox Corporation's ambitious Managed Print Services "Business Transformation" campaign, directed at mid-market technology resellers who Xerox CEO Ursula Burns saw at the time as a low-investment, low-risk vehicle for bottom-up growth of Xerox's fledgling market-moving investments in fat services companies in order to diversify out of print. The articles also appeared in the computer trade publication CRN as award-winning content on the publisher's group of industry websites. Paige Coverage in 2009 received the *Channel Citizen of the Decade* award from United Business Media, presented by Robert C. DeMarzo. Ms. Coverage holds a doctorate in applied physics from Cornell University.

ETL Industrial Publications

# "Can I Xerox That for You?"

## Contents

# Your Historical Precedent

You are the foundation of how technology will be delivered in the future.

Too heavy of an opening?

Listen: The other day I took my Jeep in for a tune-up, to the person I've learned to trust with my car: My auto mechanic. I got new spark plugs, oil, new tires, and had to sweet talk him into giving me a new inspection sticker even though my parking brake is busted (It's a 5-speed manual -- If I leave it parked in gear who needs a parking brake? Right?) I motored away happily, but also got to thinking: "I have no

Idea what brand of spark plugs he put in. And I have no clue what type of tires he put on. Or what brand of oil he poured in. And you know what? I

Don't care!

All I care about is the fact that I trust my mechanic and I pay him to take care of the rest of those important decisions."

Did you know that in 1969, the U.S. Congress conducted hearings on antitrust and monopoly issues, which included testimony that analyzed the reasons for the rapid growth of the U.S. automotive diagnostic and repair industry? (You know, the auto repair guys...)

Listen to these reasons given for the rapid rise in use, and the standardization of adoption, of the auto repair business. (For the most fun, substitute the word "vendor" when you read "dealership," which back then were more closely tied to the brand manufacturers than they are today.)

1) Customers did not trust the automobile dealerships (AKA "the vendors") to reliably service their cars.

2) Customers thought the dealers did not have well-trained mechanics.

3) Customers thought the primary interest of auto dealers was selling new cars vs. delivering service for existing cars.
In addition, of those who preferred to go to a dealer for service, "only
3 percent said it was because of good personal experience with the dealer."

Sound familiar? It does, doesn't it?

You give better service than any of the vendors you sell. And if you ask me, here we see a clear historical precedent to support the expectation that managed print and technology service providers will soon become institutionalized in the minds of all customers as the best and most logical way to purchase, deploy and service technology.

Mass-market reliance on the U.S. automotive diagnostic and repair industry became popularly institutionalized in the mid-1900s for reasons like those that motivate today's customers to employ the expertise of technology solution providers.

So right there you have it. There's your clear historical parallel that suggests the technology solution provider channel will continue to become more pervasive, and that a broader mainstream group of customers will grow to rely upon it and continue to rely upon it generation after generation.

## If Only Detroit Had Risked Cannibalization

Lazy journalists who blow great news hooks because they snooze past them waiting to be awoken by corporate platitudes really stick in my craw.

Allow me to explain: I commence a wholesale deletion of my browser bookmarks every month or so and nearly nuked this jewel from

Reuters, which hit late March.

Now I know why I saved it.

The reporter, Franklin Paul (God bless him; sure, he's a great guy, love peace and happiness to all), and his editors (get 'em boys …) think they're on to something by suggesting that Xerox's accelerated R&D ambitions could somehow create print solutions so excellent that they might displace other Xerox machines already on the job.

Writing about Xerox's ColorQube solid ink ambitions, the reporter tells us that "Oddly enough, (Get it? He writes for Reuters) ColorQube can replace laser printers, those workhorse models found in a multitude of offices--many made by Xerox."

If this is supposed to frighten investors, then let's all have a quick reality check here, folks: Those Xerox machines already on the job that are being replaced--well, we hate to break it to Franklin Paul, but they are being replaced by--guess what?--Xerox machines. This was the headline: "Xerox keeps up R&D, risks cannibalization" And here was the lead:

NEW YORK (Reuters) - Eyeing a chance to bear down on its rivals, Xerox plans to keep up the pace of spending on research and development, even if it means cannibalizing some of its products as customers rethink their choices about office equipment. Now, what if, say 10 or 15 years ago (or even five), we saw this same headline and lead graph, except instead of Xerox, it read like this: "GM keeps up R&D, risks cannibalization"

NEW YORK (Reuters) - Eyeing a chance to bear down on its rivals, General Motors plans to keep up the pace of spending on research and development, even if it means cannibalizing some of its products as customers rethink their choices about automobiles. Don't you think the world might be a better place today?

ELL Industrial Publications

# Strange Days

"At the start of June, the sun rises in the constellation of Taurus; at the end of June, the sun rises in the constellation of Gemini." I don't know what that means but I do know that at the start of each June, things begin to get strange. The strangeness arrives in all forms, spanning the glorious and the insane. Sometimes it comes as genius. Other times, neglect.

New York City cab drivers just began taking credit cards with a smile.

Deli clerks just began forgetting to put mayo on sandwiches served already quartered and tooth-picked. Anyway, it finds a feed tray, the strangeness always gets fed at the start of June.

Are you ready for the CandyFab 6000? If you thought cost-per-page printing broke down the barriers to print, wait 'til the office staffs at your customer sites get their thumbs on the "print" button of this sweet addition to the fleet. The CandyFab 6000 really is a printer in the sense that it combines a fixed set of primary ingredients into repeatable (albeit 3-D) physical products than can be handled (and digested, like the secret plans they're coming through the door for).

The CandyFab 6000's toner is sugar in various forms and colors, and just writing about this delicious invention is going straight to my thighs.

Here's something else strange: The May 28 issue of The New England
Journal of Medicine says chemicals in point-of-sale receipt printers may be causing cashiers to come down with asthma. Serious stuff, because Lord knows it's tough enough having to be a cashier in the first place. But I'll let you be the judge of this one. Any story that has a quote that reads: "Many people sneeze just when opening the morning newspaper" gives me the creeps.

"Four-year-old Molly was still giddy with excitement over the guinea pig she'd had for less than two days, when she fed it to the computer printer."

I didn't make that one up.

Yes, two-month-old "Meemo" (apparently a Guinea pig) slipped into a printer in the blink of an eye. "We shook it upside down and thought it wasn't in there, but then we saw a paw peeking out so we called for help," said dad, Gordon.
Needless to say, it was a close one.
Strange enough for ya?

## Waste Not, Want Not

Here's something the late Arte Johnson would have found both interesting, and stupid.

It's the new RITI printer powered by coffee, just like the rest of us. The RITI printer "operates without any electricity or the need to buy ink. You place the coffee grounds on the top of the printer via the ink case and move (some lever) left and right to print. No electricity needed, but it only prints in black and white and is not meant for large jobs."

Not meant for large jobs. And what a waste of good (or bad) coffee beans. At least your documents will smell like you were working.

Keep going!

## Don't Try to Reason with Us

Remember that hilarious moment back in the late 1990s when chip maker AMD tried to bow out of direct, racetrack competition with
Intel over the rival chip maker's rapidly increasing, bare-knuckle GHz speeds (which AMD almost barely ... but couldn't keep up with)?
The AMD plan was to de-emphasize processor clock speeds by mishmashing their value into a formula of other factors at the board and
I/O levels that ended up producing what AMD simply dubbed the "Performance Rating."
A pal of mine who worked for AMD in its Texas HQ during this time remembers "a mass cultural hallucination" inside AMD's

marketing department. How could a single-focus Intel chip with flames painted on its side possibly compete with a sophisticated AMD chip bearing a performance benchmark that's Harvard Law compared to Intel's greased lightning.

The AMD "Performance Rating" campaign failed to satisfy computer users, who at the time were discovering the Internet, running more processor-intensive games and applications, and generally so sick of watching that spinning hourglass that the faster the processor the better — at least as a starting point to performance.

Well, move over AMD and enter Canon, the printer maker who thinks now's a good time to abandon "page-per-minute" ratings for a new printer output metric based on how quickly a printer can produce a standard CMYK image that all printer makers must use to benchmark their output speeds.

"It's called 'images per minute,' and it calls for a standardized test pattern to be used in lieu of the old 'print whatever you want' system that was the hallmark of the 'pages per minute' measurement," the story tells us. Why will this effort by Canon fail? Well, the story suggests things aren't going so well already: "So far, no major manufacturer has switched its ratings from ppm to ipm across the board; even Canon hasn't changed all of its printers' specs to ipm ratings."

But here's the real reason images per minute will never catch on, and it's the opposite of processor speed: No one really cares about page-per-minute ratings anyway, so why switch?

Notes:

_____

_____

_____

_____

_____

_____

 Be sure to write down important numbers!

1. _____

2. _____

3. _____

4. _____

5. _____

6. _____

7. _____

8. _____

9. _____

10. _____

 Now let's talk about money!

# An Easy Extra $48,000 a Year

I'll keep this one short and simple.

In addition to your current proposal volume, if you added just one additional quote per day, valued at only $1,000, you would add $48,000 in annual revenue based on a 20 percent win rate.

My Continuing War Against Analysts Continues

OK maybe I shouldn't call it a war. But as you loyal readers have witnessed, there are few things I enjoy more than calling out pompous, poorly informed, late-to-the-party tech industry analysts. Submitted for your approval: Gartner vice president of research Ken Weilerstein speaking at the annual Print & Imaging Summit in Los Angeles this week.

Struggling to make sense, Weilerstein bantered on about cloud-based printing saving folks money; printer consolidation serving the same purpose as server consolidation, and how it's important to save electricity.

The payoff of Weilerstein's vision: A 30 percent cut in the hard cost of office printing. Why not a 50 percent reduction in overall print costs? Why not take that trendy cloud idea and translate it into a centralized managed print platform that meters devices remotely?

Oh, and the consolidation idea. If Weilerstein read the comments made at the beginning of this year by Gary Gillam, Xerox's vice president of channel operations for the North American Reseller Organization, then Weilerstein not only waited too long to parrot Gillam's comments in public, but he also lost everything in translation.

The term Weilerstein should have used is asset-optimization. Instead of just reducing a client's overall print hardware footprint by replacing stand-alone printers, copiers and fax machines with fewer high-margin MFPs, asset optimization aligns a customer's still-reliable printing assets with select additions of new equipment and services.

The larger goal: Maximize productivity and reduce costs with a minimum initial investment.

I'll cease fire, for now.

# Device Creep

Every so often we return to the vault and dust off a little jewel of wisdom that still applies to profitable managed print services.

Today's flashback: Device creep.

David Brownlee, president of CAMCorpUSA, a managed print provider in Pinckney, Mich., recalls asking a new customer how many printers the business had. The customer remembered five of them, but when Brownlee did a full inventory, seven times that amount was the final tally.

"When you walked down an aisle, you would almost trip over them, there were so many," Brownlee remembers.
Most of the rogue printers were small inkjets that burned through expensive consumables without any central cost-management strategy.

Solution providers across the country say upward of 75 percent of all new customers operate far too many printers in relation to their staffing levels and, in turn, incur excessive costs and inefficiencies.
What's the antidote to device creep?

Don't let customers (if possible) just add new printers from you, and
(no matter what) don't let them go out and buy their own.

Manage the print network under a single cost structure, add the right machines based on departmental need and headcount, and be creative about end-lifing or supporting non-Xerox (there, I said it) printers.

I know a managed print provider who offers full management and coverage of non-networked printers. These are devices attached via
USB ports which don't deliver networked reporting features like paper consumption or toner usage. What this fellow does is simply

charge $80 a year for each unmanaged printer, and if one fails, he just buys the customer another one. In other words, he just rolls the dice.

Guess what. He tells me 80 percent of each of those $80-per-year billings is pure profit.

## Another Reason They Call It Green

Did you know 38 percent of U.S. travelers will pay more to travel companies that protect the environment?

Hang on, it gets better. Those travelers who'll pay more for green goods and services will pay up to 10 percent more, says the Travel
Industry of America.

Flashback to early 2009. A landscape architect named Nick Overall is honored as the Norwalk Tree Alliance's Tree Advocate of the Year.

The appreciative Mr. Overall said news of the award immediately attracted new business from conservation-minded customers.

*If You've Got It, Flaunt It.*

There's a fun toy I want you to have.

It's the Xerox Sustainability Calculator, and it gives you a visual way to see how much of a reduction in energy, greenhouse gases and solid waste you can achieve by optimizing a customer's print environment.

It really drives home the value of ENERGY STAR certified printers too. Boy do they make a difference!

Look, even if you don't care about conservation – yes, we know you're out there, and it's OK -- missing the opportunity to showcase a green attribute can mean lost business.

You don't have to believe in global warming to shake the hand of a walk-in customer who noticed the sign you placed in the window that says "Your green printing resource."

Xerox partners don't have to make this stuff up.(I know, I know... "Oh, here we go again with the Xerox pitch..."). But really, 80 percent of Xerox's qualified products already met or exceeded the ENERGY STAR standard two years ago, and the company's goal is to take that figure to 90 percent by 2010.

ENERGY STAR products can save a small business that spends $2,000 a year on energy bills over 30 percent - or about $700 per year, with no sacrifice in performance.

In fact, if all computers sold in the U.S. were ENERGY STAR certified, the country would save $2 billion a year, and reduce greenhouse gas emissions equal to 2 million cars, according to ENERGY STAR.

And Xerox as a company sets a pretty good example, too -- one that customers who opt for green suppliers will appreciate: Xerox cut companywide greenhouse gas emissions by 20 percent between 2002 to 2008, and Xerox aims to take that figure to 45 percent by 2012. More than 90 percent of Xerox paper meets requirements for a sustainable paper cycle.

Xerox achieved an internal recycle rate of 92 percent in 2008.

Here's the Sustainability Calculator! Have fun! http://www.consulting.xerox.com/flash/thoughtleaders/suscalc/xeroxCalc.html

# More Tools Than A Hooters at Happy Hour

Tell me! When will IT analysts stop confusing things for everyone?

Yeah, that's what I said.

Xerox brings to market its Enterprise Print Services (EPS) solution this week and the leading analysts at InfoTrends aggressively freak out.

Pretty much all that's happened with EPS is this: Xerox is demonstrating that it's aware that fewer and fewer workers who need to hit the print button are shackled to a desk in an office. So

Xerox did something about it, rolling out support for home and virtual printing, adding print routing features to save money, paper and time, and making it easier to keep more print jobs in-house versus sending them out.

You wouldn't know this listening to the Chicken Littles at InfoTrends, who, upon learning that EPS enables Xerox to assist in managing and negotiating commercial print strategies with third-party shops on behalf of partners, reacted in a shocking fit of animal paranoia.

"This clearly could raise concern to print service providers (PSPs), many of whom are loyal Xerox customers," InfoTrends howled, immediately back-tracking on this dire threat by saying managed print opportunities for everyone remain strong.

Upon hearing that EPS has print-from-smartphone capabilities as part of its virtual environment support, InfoTrends leapt into a four-alarm panic over the proposition that EPS could soon pack more tools than a Hooters at happy hour.

"Should we, therefore, expect a maelstrom of new document solutions that addresses this growing segment, either supporting the users' remotely connected MFPs or mobile devices?"

Calm down boys. Software happens.

And so, it seems, does unwarranted fear.

# You Were Born at The Right Time

I don't hear it much anymore, but I remember that for a while there it was fashionable conversation to ask mind-bending, out-of-place-intime- and-space questions like, "What if Mozart was born in the Stone
Age, before there was any such thing as a piano, or perhaps even music?"

Easy to see how this made for great cocktail conversations, right?

Of course there's a cart-and-horse element that spoils this "Twilight Zone" scenario, thanks to John Locke and his tabula rasa blank slate. Still, something deep inside each of us does seem to respond positively to the suggestion that the epoch we occupy is the one we were specifically outfitted for in the factory.

As we tumble into 2010, "the rate of business model change from traditional break-and-fix IT support to managed services will accelerate faster than at any time in the past several years, moving into double digits," according to the Institute for Partner Education & Development (IPED). The reason: Managed services lower customer costs, reduce waste and equipment failure, and provide a reliable recurring revenue stream for managed service providers.

Managed print is no exception, so if you're thinking of embarking on a managed print services business and wondering if now is the right time, it is.

# Don't Hire Anyone
# Until You Read This

Even if you're not specifically in managed print services (naughty

you!) this information is vital if you plan to hire salespeople who'll be

selling any form of managed service that departs from break-and-fix or project-based work.

A few weeks ago, I spoke of two types of salespeople: Hunters and

Farmers.

A hunter wants to move in for the kill, then move on.
A farmer wants to manage the account over a longer period of time.
Farmers sell managed print services better than hunters, because the right message is in place from the start.

But hunters can sell managed print too. The question here is, how then do you manage the account without bringing in another body?

The answer is this: If you have hunters who close deals, you need farmers to eventually come in and manage the account.
Farmers can sell, but they do not have to be salespeople, and don't need to be compensated at the same level as a salesperson.

From a customer relationship standpoint, one strategy is to let a hunter help manage an account for the first three months, then hand the account over to a farmer. You may already have a farmer on staff who can do this.

None of this matters, of course, if you can't close deals. The best managed services salespeople don't come from a box-pusher background, and they don't even have to understand technology all that much.

The best managed services salespeople are folks who have sold insurance, advertising and other intangibles. This is what you should look for when hiring salespeople to sell your managed services.
People who can articulate and sell things that have ROI beyond the physical addition of a product.

Next step: The question now becomes, how do you pay this new salesperson when it will likely take a year for them to build up a new customer base that pays enough of an annuity to adequately compensate them, plus provide new incentive?

You give them a first-year salary guarantee monitored by 90-day reviews.

For example (and this is a real example), if you are selling Xerox
Managed Print services as a PagePack Partner, with as few as a hundred or so C-Level prospects and a modest proposals-per-month rate and equally modest close rate at 25 percent commission, a good salesperson can bring down six figures by the end of their third year.

The salary draw you gave them will be well paid back by then too.

Exact formulas on the way.

# How to Make $239,598:
# A Real Managed Print Formula for You

I recently claimed that with as few as a hundred C-Level prospects, a modest proposals-per-month rate, and an equally modest close rate at a 25 percent commission, a new managed print salesperson can bring down six figures by the end of their third year on the job, and that the first-year salary draw you'll need to front them to get on their feet will be well paid back by then too.

I also promised some real numbers to back that claim up, and I'll give them to you now. Afterwards, I think you'll see that the reason I tout Xerox (I'm actually not a Xerox employee) and their PagePack managed print offering is because they have a real profit formula that makes you money better than any model I've ever seen.

Sharpen a pencil and let's do some quick math.

We need our new managed print salesperson to close four PagePack deals a month; that's the goal. In one year, that yields 48 new accounts. So let's round that up to 50 for simplicity's sake and get started.

These are all midmarket accounts for, say, the average seat count at 30 per customer, giving us 1,500 managed seats. Now divide that by 5 (because the average ratio of printers to employees is 4.4, remember?) and we get 300 printing devices under management. Now, the ratio of color to B&W printers is typically 1-to-5, so we have 60 color printers and 240 B&W printers across all 50 accounts. Multiply the 60 color printers by 0.2, and the 240 B&W printers by 0.8 so we back some cost out to cover program overhead. That leaves us with a figure of 12 for the color systems, and 192 for the B&W ones.

Still with me?

Now, multiply the 12 color printers by the average monthly pages printed by a color device (2,500) and you get 30,000. Multiply that by a fixed cost per page (regardless of toner coverage!) of 0.10, and you get 3,000. That color printer is going to generate an average of 1,500 B&W pages per month, too, so also multiply the 12 color printers by 1,500, and multiply the resulting 18,000 pages by the fixed B&W cost of 0.015, which yields 270. Add the 270 to the 3,000 and your monthly revenue from the color systems is $3,270.

Then take the 192 B&W printers and multiply that times the average monthly print output of a B&W printer (4,000) and you get 768,000 pages, times the B&W page cost of 0.015 and you're making $11,520 a month from the B&W systems. Add that to the $3,270, giving you

$14,790 a month, plus your 35% markup times 12 months, and your annual managed print revenue from the 50 midsize customers your new sales person bagged in year-one is $239,598. Imagine where you'll be by year three?!

Now, take that salesperson out to dinner, will ya?

## Yes, You Can Close One Deal a Week

An old high school teacher of mine used to remind us that for every hand raised with a question, another five hands are too afraid to go up.

A brave hand went up this week wondering how on earth a salesperson could keep on track to close four medium-size PagePack deals a month. That's the close rate I proposed in my "How to make $239,598" blog, which gave the math on how to hit that level of recurring managed print revenue in just one year.

What helps my people hit this quota is the fact that when it comes to any competitive open bid for managed print services, Xerox always gets invited to the dance. Customers always want to hear what we as

Xerox partners have to say, and what our number is.

And believe me when I tell you: All we have to be is close, not the lowest bid. Just close. Because customers typically opt for the Xerox brand name and will pay a premium not to feel like they're being experimented on like a lab rat. Same reason people ask for a Band-Aid or a Kleenex – both trademarks and generic nouns. Xerox is print.

People know it.

Practicing what you preach also helps close down deals. We run

PagePack internally and follow the wisdom of Gary Gillam, Xerox's vice president of channel operations for the North American Reseller Organization.

Gary will tell you that if you get your own managed print platform in order and have your numbers to share with customers, you can open up a managed print pitch by saying, "I want to come in and share with you what we've done with our own business. ... So you essentially become a case study for the benefits. In short, the expert user becomes the user's expert."

Boy I love that line.

## I'm Gonna Rope Me
## One of Those HP Printers

So I was in Dallas Tuesday riding along with a fellow managed print peddler when he suddenly whipped the steering wheel hard right sending our car barreling down an exit towards a large, unmarked truck parked in front of a single-story office building.

As we screeched to a halt, he jumped from the driver's side while the car was practically still skidding and hollered at two young fellas unloading what were clearly brand-new Xerox printers.

"Remember, get the HP systems out of there!" he yells at the lads.
"Don't ask anyone in there; just unplug them and throw them in the back of the truck. Re-network the users."

"You know these guys?" I ask him stepping out of the car.

"They're mine," he replies. "We picked up this account last month.
Twelve new printers and a three-year contract. But the HP boxes have to go. I refuse to feed them."

You see, my friend here is not certified to offer full-fleet management through Xerox's PagePack FM managed print service – at least not yet.

No, he's a successful Xerox PagePack managed print partner who plans to get full-fleet certified ASAP, but until then, he has another way of dealing with third-party printer management.

"Switch them out and roll back the cost. Don't even tell the customer.
Just say we are consolidating for cost savings," he tells me.

"What do you do with the old HP printers?" I asked.

He laughed. "Target practice," he said. "I've got 10 acres outside of Ft. Worth. I've covered them with gas and set them ablaze. It's the only way to make HP toner carts melt like a Xerox solid ink system."
Texans.

Anyway, we're standing there as an HP printer hits the back of the truck with an ugly thud and one of the boys walks up and says, "You should come inside and see this. We don't know what to do."

Inside, in a large supply closet, we're shown a wall of unopened cases of HP toner. The kid starts counting them as my friend grimaces.

"This is how I sold them on PagePack, but they didn't tell me they were hiding this stuff," he says. "Xerox ships solid ink direct and we price per page, not by toner coverage. All this crap in here was probably ordered by four different secretaries each afraid to run out of toner. What a waste."

"About a hundred," the kid says of the number of HP toner cases stuffed in the closet. "Maybe more."

And that is simply not funny, unless you're Mark Hurd. Law Enforcement And Marketing I've heard it said that marketing is a bit like law enforcement. In law enforcement, there can never be too little crime, so effort needs to be judged by input, not necessarily output.

Same goes for marketing. You can never really have too many sales, so everything about marketing is input. If sales slump, the last thing you want is any indication that marketing fell short.

This is why I was thrilled at the results of our last Business Transformation poll, which asked: "What percent of your managed Print revenue do you put back into marketing?"

A third of those who chimed in said they reinvest 4 percent or less of their managed print revenues back into marketing efforts (cue the applause sign). But the golden number was 67 percent. That's how many said they reinvest between 9 percent and 12 percent of their managed print revenues back into marketing efforts (cue balloon drop).

Now, it just so happens that Best-in-Class solution providers (that Top 30 percent of the bunch, according to IPED) invest on average 11 percent of their total revenues into marketing activities, which is 56 percent more than the industry average.

This says a lot about the caliber and marketing savvy of the managed print providers and solution providers who took our poll.

Great job!

Print VARs: Should We Fight to Stay Small?

If you're a small, local printer parts and services dealer who feels threatened by the acquisition of Affiliated Computer Services by
Xerox because you're worried you'll eventually lose business to a big guy, relax.

Sure Xerox wants more customers. Don't you?
Here's one horror story that popped up in this community about a Xerox buyout of a local print dealer:

"They (Xerox/GI) recently bought one near me. The impact on the small local VARs was immediate. Even the two fellows I know that sell remanufactured toner cartridges have been pinched by this company, in only 6 months! This will definitely impact small local
VARs."

Don't know the exact details, but I do know this. That local print dealer sold themselves to Xerox. They could have said no. Besides, the threat is not consolidation; it's a superior managed print model. When you offer a managed print service that allows customers to forget about device management, toner cost and shipping, third-party printers, and a plethora of other messy, costly and planet threatening headaches, smart businesspeople are going to migrate to your managed print services.

Sure a small guy making money from remanufactured toner cartridges is going to get pinched, because the most efficient managed print service model takes toner cost out of the equation as a standalone expense and prices on a per-page basis, regardless of toner coverage.

The managed print model I speak of is PagePack 3.0 from – you guessed it – Xerox. And yes, PagePack 3.0 is designed to capture all of a customer's print business, from deployment to support. So the question here really becomes: Why aren't you the one taking business from weaker competitors? Why aren't you a Xerox partner?

Speaking of questions, many of you took a crack at our Business
Transformation Question of the Week last week: What is the average employee-to-printer ratio in a large business?
The correct answer: 4.4 (and thanks go to Jim Salzer of DocuAudit International for that great stat).

# Get Your Freak On: Xerox Buys ACS

This was the Deal Journal entry in today's Wall Street Journal Online:

Mergers & Acquisitions: Game changer? Xerox agreed to pay $6.4 billion in cash and stock for outsourcing and information-services company Affiliated Computer Services.

This deal is brilliantly enormous and so intelligent that it would require the frozen brain of Stanislaw Lem to understand its total ROI.

Let me make this simple.

ACS has the guts to turn nothing down.

That's not an absolute, but it's the freaking truth when it comes to execution philosophy.

I'm standing up right now. I'm not seated. I'm so damn emotional about this I'm going to write like Hemingway. Someone told me once he wrote standing up. I never believe that crap.

You can deliver anything you want when you do business with vendor and service partners that you can motivate, and have deliver to you perks and MDF funds. OnForce can provide feet on the street. Xerox can deliver managed print services. All together now, name your favorite remote monitoring platform..?

You can say to vendors "Hey, I have these customers you have to go through me to get to."

You can be ACS.

Tell your banker you're going to milk your vendor and disty partners for all they're worth on a major expansion campaign. Meet with each separately. When everyone shares proof you'll be:

A) Embarking on a major IT services expansion driven by vendor participation and back funding
B) The only one in the room who had the guts to say "can we do this thing or not?"

## Always Leave Your Mark

I've always loved thick textbooks and that rich smell they have after being used.

That inky red "USED" stamp college bookstores smack on the edges of previously owned textbooks was always a message to me that there was more information to be found inside than when the text was originally published.

Whatever one thinks of them, yellow highlighter marks, notations scribbled alongside paragraphs, and folded page corners indicating the most important section of a 30-page chapter all serve as traffic that makes a path more easily traveled.

Used books are less expensive? I'd pay a premium for the copy with a pen mark on page 22 reminding me to see page 238 for the stuff I'll need to know for the test.

This leftover anxiety from college resurfaced when it hit me that a way to more randomly (and dastardly) mark up and save notations on digital school textbooks might not make a bad application overlay to a collaborative platform like Xerox's DocuShare Enterprise Content

Management (ECM) system.

Schools are using ECM to remove paper-based processes ranging from textbook chapters to homework assignments — all of which are accessed online and printed when it's time (like when the kid is at home, so they don't have to lug around a book or crumple printed homework in a backpack).

All genius. But atop this collaborative framework, a bad-boy little application that might even let you make fun of a teacher could take the digital process of dissecting information out of a vacuum, so hand-me-down notes from pupils who came before you don't get lost.

Any ISVs out there listening?

"Any ISVs out there listening?"

---------------------------------------------------------------------------

📎 "Yes, I'm listening!"

Name: _____

Title: _____

Today's date: _____

Time: _____

## Controlled Substances?

When I worked nightshifts in college feeding paper behind a 5-color
Heidelberg offset printing press, there was this dream I had each and every morning.

It was one of those dreams where it's neither day, nor night. Just that gray color in between. I could fly around in this dream if I wanted, but what was happening on the ground was more interesting. In this dream I no longer had to worry about running up along the side the gargantuan printing press (the size of a UPS delivery truck) to flip the water dampeners that regulate and feed water to the plates of each ink tower on the press. In this dream, if I had a proper ink mix and a plate fit, I was good to go.

From the www.whattheythink.com:

"According to the Waterless Printing Association, the average 6-color, 40-inch printing press utilizes 3175 gallons of fresh water each year. Waterless printing saves this precious resource. Furthermore, because the chemicals used in fountain solution are 'controlled substances, used fountain solution becomes a waste stream that must be collected and treated to avoid environmental damage. Fountain solutions also emit Volatile Organic Compounds (VOCs), which have been linked to reduced local air quality as well as smog and ozone layer damage."

Waterless printing. This is my dream come true. The plates cost an arm and a leg but we're talking about ending a battle that's been going on since the dawn of offset printing.

My heart gravitated to digital printers the day I was introduced to the solid ink system from Xerox, which operates in an offset print-style manner.

But I get a pinch of nostalgia for big (or small) offset presses when I can remember them without the thought of having to maintain an ink/water balance.

Some Great Advice to Remember

Here's some great advice we got several months ago from Gary Gillam, Xerox's vice president of channel operations for the North American Reseller Organization. It's well worth breaking back out as we head into fall.

Basically, Gary told us that when we practice what we preach, we can do a whole lot more business.

Think about it. You've got a stubborn customer shaking his head at the idea of spending a little money for your print asset optimization service? Why not help this customer see the value of something like asset optimization through your own experience with it?

Use yourself and your business as a case study.

Assess your own print capabilities and transform them to become more efficient.

Then try this opener with a customer: "I want to come in and share with you what we've done with our own business."

Poof! Your customer now understands you share the same challenges and opportunities they do, and this makes it clear you understand their business needs too.

Gary says it best: "You, the expert user, will suddenly become the user's expert."

That's poetry, ladies and gents.

Oh, and so before we go and while we're on the subject of marketing, check out these great marketing tips from Beth Ann Kilberg-Walsh, manager of marketing communications at Xerox.

Beth tells us that "customization and personalization should be a priority" in marketing, and she runs through a whole list of things that can improve the success of your own marketing campaigns!

# You Don't Even Have to Read This

I think the term "Podcast" was a total mistake and part of the reason audio-only presentations delivered over consumer devices will struggle for years to come (unless they are for children).

The term, feel and sound of "Podcast" reeks of classic, shortsighted Silicon Valley euphoria. Its pretentious "short for iPod" branding pegs its existence to a single operating system. Everything about it alienates more than invites.

That said, below is a link to what -- I wish -- used to be called a

"Podcast."

Listening to it will be like putting 100-octane gasoline in your engine.

It is one of the most hard-core enterprise managed print statements

I've ever heard, and pulls no punches when it comes to the real truth about telling a customer who to trust, who has the real background and references, and who really knows what's going on and how to make money in managed print. It's enterprise hard core. SMB customers will get it immediately.

Check it out. It's a minute or so long: http://bit.ly/25R8KJ

Oh, So Long Ago

Greg Walters is my new favorite person because he leveraged this

community to call me out on my recent trashing of the brand name "Podcast" with a snappy riposte that proved both our points.

I was cursing the term "Podcast" as a total failure of epic proportion (you can read the rant in its entirety here), then in jumped Greg, making this colorful point:

"OK - let me get this straight - somebody from 'Xerox' is miffed, albeit in jest, over the word/brand 'Podcast'"? The same Xerox that for years would have their field reps ask receptionists all over the world,

"...could you Xerox a copy of this for me please?"

Leaping lizards!

Greg's point goes right to the heart of my Aug. 3 post about how excellent it is that the proper noun "Xerox" also acts as a verb in the poetic sea of American idiomatic expressions. I go off in a tangent about Jack Trout of Trout & Partners but you can read it all later in the book.

# You Know the Answer

Before we get cracking, two students from Kingston University in
London have created a video by filming carefully positioned printers printing, then accelerating the projection by about 9,000 times. You know that's cool.

Your answers to our last "Question of the Week" told me you also know your customers will print more if color costs the same per page as black and white. (That was the exact question, by the way. Thanks to all who rang in!).

There should be no cost difference between color and B&W. That's the way customers behave anyhow. Mr. Print Button is color-blind, and rightly so. Look at it this way. Toner cartridge pricing is typically based on something like 5 percent sheet coverage, which yields an industry average price per page based on 20 percent toner coverage
(20 percent being the multiple of 5 percent each of red, blue, yellow and black (CMYK)).

So if you contract your managed cost-per-page print estimate on this standard 20 percent coverage, you can get into a heap of trouble very quickly if customers begins to exceed that coverage on a regular basis, which they will – all the time.

In fact, they won't be able to stop themselves.

Customers who enter into managed print agreements immediately see the value of having new, high-end multifunction printers available, so they task them with printing work they previously may have sent outside, like full-color marketing material. When this happens, your pre-contract managed print assessment designed to tell you how much on average a customer prints will suddenly be way off, and if you based your contract on 20 percent coverage, you'll likely find yourself buying a whole lot of toner out of your own pocket.

You know that doesn't fly.

## Good Deeds Float Forever

Life is precious, and escapes us every instant.

My advice: Love, believe in one another and work your butt off.

Robert Banks was the long-time general counsel at Xerox before retiring in 1989. He died last week at age 75.

"Banks' reputation as a hard-nosed lawyer hell-bent on changing how in-house and outside counsel worked together started in 1976, when he took over the legal department at Xerox. He believed the company had too many lawyers, spent too much money and abdicated too much responsibility to outside law firms. "When I took over, it was clear to me that we were, if you will, in the hands of outside counsel,' Banks told The American Lawyer in 1989, when the magazine named him one of the 10 most influential lawyers of the decade.

"So Banks got to work. He cut his in-house staff from 150 to 66, and made sure those 66 lawyers were good enough to handle the bulk of

Xerox's work. He started a contest for Xerox's outside work, doling it out to more than 100 law firms instead of relying on the few the company had been blindly loyal to for years.

"Once he established that doing Xerox's legal work was a privilege,

Banks reversed course and announced the company would work with only a few firms -- those that could provide the best value at the lowest cost.

"The results were, by all accounts, astounding. He trimmed Xerox's legal spend from $45 million in 1976 (measured using 1988 dollars) to

$23 million in 1988, and brought 80 percent of the company's legal work in-house."

# The Guy Who Showed Me That Seeing Is Believing

I'm here at Everything Channel's XChange 09 event in Washington,

D.C., where many things are very hot, especially the weather, which is a sweltering 94 humid degrees.

It's a hot show too (in the good sense of the word), with hundreds of Solution Providers getting the chance to lay their hands of the newest of the new technologies, and rap with vendor channel reps about "what's in it for me?" Which is always the way to begin a vendor discussion, no?

So I grab a glass of cold chardonnay as I enter the Vendor Solution

Pavilion, and what do I see but the Xerox booth, manned by the very compelling Guy Summers, who's Xerox's Partner Manager for D.C. and Northern Virginia.

Guy is typing something into a laptop when I reach him and introduce myself, and what he's doing is something each and every one of you should have seen -- and should still see.

He has a little spread sheet called "Turning Pages into Recurring
Revenue and Margin," which as a title alone is a very compelling idea all to itself. In this spread sheet, he shows me how if I enter in my number of Xerox PagePack 3.0 managed print customers, and the average printing user seats per customer, I can calculate my total recurring revenue per month from my PagePack 3.0 customer base, plus my 35 percent margin add-on, and get a total for the recurring managed print revenue I'll see in a year.

Here's the first one I tried: 27 customers, an average of 8 seats per customer (I'm pretending to be a small shop), and with color priced at .10 cents per page and B&W practically negligible (because PagePack breaks down barriers to printing in color), I bring in $4,428 per month from these customers, including my markup of 35 percent (a cool
$1,550), then multiply that total figure by 12 and I'm banking $18,598 a year from my Xerox PagePack 3.0 managed print customer base.

Change the 8 seat average to 18, and the end result figure jumps to
$41,845 a year in recurring revenue (get 'em under contracts folks).

These numbers are just averages to whet your whistle, Guy explains to me, as he turns my attention to a "Reseller Profit" quote from

PagePack 3.0's actual OneQuote system (meaning this is the real thing now, no more "averages." We're working from actual numbers off a

Xerox Phaser 8860/PP.)

Based on a three year PagePack 3.0 contract, if a customer chews through 5,000 color prints per month at my cost of .03 cents per page,

Xerox charges me $171 a month, while I charge the customer $549 a month -- a 175.45 percent profit margin over the three-year contract.

That, folks, is very, very HOT.

**Your Question of The Week, Examined**

Something of a cultural divide once separated the camps of information technology and telecommunications.

Before network intelligence moved to the edge and IP eliminated the need for switchboard operators, you staked your flag in either camp based on what you were more familiar with: The Seven-layer OSI model, or how to configure a PBX.

So when we saw the results of last week's Question of the Week (you can find it on the home page) your responses reminded us that managed print was actually a third camp of professionals, outside those containing the IT guys and the telco folks.

Remember? It was the copier guy with the leasing contract and the suitcase of calibration tools who was really the guy dealing with all those reams of paper a customer would chew up, not the IT guy.

I'll let Greg, who responded to last week's Question, put it in his own very articulate words:

"For decades the printers were sold as a commodity, if not an oddity.

And trying to mix 'copier guys' selling with 'IT guys' order-taking is a cultural challenge. But separating and allowing the managed print service provider to stumble and grow seems to be working. As well as establishing 'legitimacy' with the propeller-heads of the IT world."

Thanks, Greg. I like the way you put that.

Oh, and last week's question also revealed that two-thirds of you who responded were running managed services (IT) before looking at managed print services.

# My Action Hero Meets Einstein

In all my favorite action movies there's always this one guy -- he can be a good guy or a bad guy, it doesn't matter -- who has some special skill, but who's also really cool and sits productively, quietly in the background until something happens that requires him to jump into action.

And when he does, he is The Baddest Mutha in The Valley.

To me, LED printers are that one freakin' cool guy I'm talking about.

Unlike laser or ink-jet printers, LED printers are the Jedi Knights of the print galaxy because they pack light-emitting diodes as print heads, which carve perfect images and stay calibrated much longer than delicate mirror-dependent laser print heads. With no moving parts in their print heads, LED printers are reliable as heck and can haul butt when it comes to chewing up a big print job.

And speaking of speed...

What's always been sort of a cosmic speed limit for LED printers has just been broken with the introduction of a new line of Xerox

WorkCentre 7400 series systems -- LED printers, the lot of them.

The Einsteinium rule of thumb has been that LED printers have a resolution limitation based on the physical number of LEDs modern

fabs can pack into a print head. The formula has been roughly one-toone.

To get 300dpi resolution, you gotta stuff together 300 LEDs per inch, and so on.

But check out these WorkCentre 7400 series resolutions: 14,592 LEDs - Yes, fourteen thousand -- achieve 1200x240dpi resolution, print quality that's equivalent to, and in some cases better than, comparable laser systems.

Like the astrophysicist in the observatory said to the skeptic, don't trust me, look for yourself.

# Through the Looking Glass

If I were Alice, and this was Wonderland--that odd place on the other side of the looking glass--I would be less surprised to see a left-leaning newspaper declare a pair of corporate executives the preferred policy role models for a democratic political leader in a progressive state.

But that's just what happened, and we're not in Wonderland.

In a political climate where Big Business is simply not at its peak of admiration, this editorial page in the Rochester Democrat And

Chronicle declares that lawmakers in Albany, N.Y., "could learn a few lessons about leadership from Xerox's dynamic duo."

That dynamic duo, of course, is Xerox CEO Ursula Burns and

Chairman Anne Mulcahy.

Listen to the editorial rant-on: "Mulcahy engineered an amazing turnaround at Xerox. Now Burns must not just lead the company through the recession, but determine the right moves to future success."

"The state's elected leaders need to develop the same strategy.

Lawmakers can't just work on the immediate problem of the $2.1 billion budget gap. Yes, they passed reforms recently, but those are just baby steps. We need leaders to take giant leaps."

"As Gov. David Paterson and Albany lawmakers struggle to get the state on track, they could learn a few lessons about leadership" from
Burns and Mulcahy.

"Paterson and legislators, take note."

You know, I sorta like the way things are on the other side of the looking glass.

# Can You Xerox This for Me?

Last Sunday I had a great conversation about how cool it was that the proper noun "Xerox" also acts as a verb in the poetic sea of American idiomatic expressions.

Then on Tuesday -- true to the laws of synchronicity -- I bumble across this interview with Jack Trout, uber-egomaniac and president of marketing firm Trout & Partners.

Asked the question: "If human minds don't change, then why are marketers hell-bent on trying to change them?" Trout replied:

"Psychologists point out that people don't want to change what they believe. Xerox wanted to be a computer company not just a copier company. Customers said any Xerox machine that can't make a copy isn't a Xerox machine. Coke wanted to be 'New.' Customers said you aren't new, you are the original. Volkswagen wanted to be big and expensive. Customers said you are small, economic and reliable."

As you can see, Trout is clearly insane. But clinical insanity has never disqualified anyone from a marketing position. Trust me on that one.

If you run Trout's comments through your Decoder Ring, you discover he's a marketer bashing failed marketing campaigns, something you can be sure psychologists have a point or two to make about as well.

A successful marketing campaign can make bottled water the default choice in a country with the cleanest tap water in the world. When the success of a method like marketing can produce results that defy reason, you cannot compare successes with failures. They are two separate Universes.

Marketing campaigns that don't deliver are just the residue left behind when a business does what a business is supposed to always try and do: Expand.

Synchronicity? So I'm sitting there reading Trout's desperate cry for help when a pal IM's a link to this blog from Stephen Knight, who really gets it.

"In a nutshell, positioning is the place that a product occupies in your mind. If you cut your finger, most people will ask for, or say to themselves, 'I need a Band-Aid'. Not stopping to think that Band-Aid is actually a 'brand' name. The term has become so generic, so commonplace in everyday language that we never question the source. Most of us have also said, 'Will you 'Xerox' this document?'

There are literally dozens of paper copiers on the market, but Xerox holds a 'position' in our mind. We have applied values and attributes to these words. When you think about it, what is Xerox? It is a strange word, that's it. But Xerox Inc. has done an amazing job of positioning, of fixing this word in your mind and making it a living, breathing entity."

That, folks, is good marketing.

# Deserving of A Much Greater Prize

Several years back, the Academy of Motion Picture Arts and Sciences
(The Oscar folks) saluted Steven Spielberg with a Lifetime Achievement Award for all the remarkably wonderful films he'd made.

So Spielberg gets up there on stage and produces a little note from his tux jacket pocket, saying, "I'm going to read a list of names to you, then I'll explain the significance of everyone on the list."

If you're thinking Schindler's List, no harm or foul, but this was a list of every writer who'd ever worked on, or contributed to, a Spielberg movie script--Something incredibly important, said Spielberg, because, "If it's not on the page, it's not on the stage."

So in homage to Mr. Spielberg, I'm going to read a list of remarkable accomplishments to you, then I'll explain what everyone on the list has in common.

A group in Yukon, Okla., turned used packing binder tape from waste into energy. Used tape that hit the plant floor went to a cement kiln instead of a landfill and became a fuel source. Some 720 pounds of binder tape have been converted to energy to date.

By enabling the use of off-peak electricity for certain processes, a group in Dundalk, Ireland, realized a cost savings of $100,000 in 2008, and $175,000 in the first quarter of 2009.

After coming to grips with the overwhelming amount of packaging associated with incoming parts, a group in Webster, N.Y., did some research and found reuse/recycle applications for the material. As a result, 800,000 foam sheets, 200,000 pieces of tag board, 60,000 plastic bags, 57,000 corrugated cartons and 6,900 plastic skids have been reused or recycled--all of which would have previously hit the landfill.

Using an alternative material in an equipment cleaning process, a group in Wilsonville, Ore., saved 400 pounds of material per year from heading to a landfill, and eliminated $37,000 in labor costs. The new process also proved to be faster.

What do each of these have in common? They are all winners of the
2009 Earth Awards, which for nearly two decades has been a labor of love from Xerox.

Xerox's 16th Annual Earth Awards honored projects that collectively totaled $7.3 million in cost savings, more than 1.3 million pounds in waste elimination and 500,000KWH in energy reduction.

For 2009, there were a total of 20 award winners.

Right on.

# All Boxed Up and Ready to Sell

Being a pack rat, people ask me constantly for tidbits of research or industry data I may have tucked away.

The latest such request arrived from a loyal reader curious to know if Gartner--the research group--had a new "Magic Quadrant" for printing and imaging vendors. I always consider it flattery when asked a question easily Googled, so I did the search and found this from late 2008.

This geometrically lovely Magic Quadrant of managed print service vendors has Xerox at the tip of a Big Dipper-like constellation of other vendors in the space. High altitude in the "Leader" quadrant with
East-bound acceleration into the "Visionary" quadrant is where one wants to be in these Gartner maps, and that's just where Xerox smartly landed.

Makes sense, too, when you consider that Xerox has actually devised a way for folks like you and I to really make money on real managed print services, thanks to breakthroughs like freedom from coverage-based pricing models, no shipping costs for consumables, managed third-party printers as part of your service, environmentally friendly solid-ink systems that reduce waste, leasing options that lower a customer's up-front costs, balanced deployment strategies that lower device maintenance and power costs...(Cue the sound of a phonograph needle being dragged off a playing 33RPM record)

OK, sure, I'll give it a break…

But another thing the good folks at Gartner like to do in these exercises is highlight the "Strengths" and "Cautions" of vendors floating in the Quadrants. Unlike the Magic Quadrants, these flat lists don't inspire you to conjure up that cool 3-D ability to see vendor positioning in the same way John Cusack could envision 3-D air space as an air traffic controller in "Pushing Tin" (Right. No one saw that movie), but they do highlight some interesting points.

Xerox gets a Gartner nod to strength for how it "takes a careful and methodical approach to MPS as shown in areas such as assessment, change management, and tracking and monitoring. Not only do

Xerox's assessments follow a detailed and proven methodology, but they can extend that approach to new areas." (That's code for "What works here can work over there too.) (Can I get a "Cha-ching!", anyone?)

Oh, and Xerox's "Caution" from Gartner seems like it'll become more a problem for HP now that the do-it-all company has acquired troubled consultant EDS, who sent a lot of MPS work Xerox's way. I say give what's left of EDS a few sweaty quarters to sample HP's brand of managed print service before EDS employees begin looking at HP printers like that annoying step-uncle who entered the family through a questionable marriage.

## Your Managed Print Customers Want to Be on Vacation Too

Hi gang!

I'm back from vacation, and boy I missed you all dearly!

While I was gone, I thought constantly of you and our quest to become superior managed print providers. Don't believe me?

Check it out:

I welcomed an old college chum of mine to watch my place and feed the pets while I was away. I love doing that. So many of my old chums live outside New York these days that a few weeks of free rent next door to a subway stop that takes you to Times Square in 10 minutes can be fashioned into an exciting (and inexpensive) vacation of its own. Sure it's a sales pitch, but it keeps my plants moist and my kitty fed for free.

This old chum of mine didn't wait 24 hours before he began calling, paging, texting and even Twittering me about every challenge he faced in realtime.

Understand I love my old chum, but allow me to show you some of the actual messages he sent while I entrusted him to watch my place as I attempted to get away. (Faint hearts beware: This small sampling is all real, and in the chronological order I ignored them in.)

"Hey, the buzzer rang and I missed it, who was it supposed to be?"

"Can you recommend a Thai restaurant? Don't tell me to pick one from your flier menus."

"Both TVs are showing snow. Please respond."

"Hello?"

"Paige, this needs to work for both of us or I'm gone, like back to
Texas."

"If I had the money to do [expletive deleted], this wouldn't be an issue."

You get the idea.

I practically left him an owner's manual on my house and neighborhood, and everything was working fine when I got back home. But it got me thinking that when we deliver managed print services, a big part of the job is insulating customers from all the work we're taking off their shoulders.

A monthly or quarterly report to a managed print customer that confirms ROI is one thing. But boy oh boy, after being on vacation with my old chum at the helm of the casa, I understand more than ever before why managed print offerings that burden customers only get tested once, then never invited back.

Six Degrees of Print Protection (ala Kevin Bacon)I plan to commit some holiday downtime working out the finer points of a game I'll call Six Degrees of Print Protection. I struggled to find something that rhymed with Kevin Bacon.

In this game, any device can be linked to a Xerox printer - or print job- within six steps. Any device, and I dare say any event, not just IT related.

Let's take one for a test drive: The PC used by Brenda in the accounting department of an Idaho bakery, and the picture Janet just got emailed to her Florida office from her mother in New Jersey.

Janet prints the picture to a managed Xerox printer, then (thanks to a new deal announced this week) ConnectWise software automates data collection, reporting and invoicing for the managed Xerox printers in Janet's office. Through a solution provider, ConnectWise interfaces with a Level Platforms MSP remote monitoring platform to digest data from customer monitoring systems, field technician schedules, help-desk logs and other time-tracking systems, and Level Platforms also sees that the available RAM on Brenda's PC is suddenly too low.

What was that? Four degrees? Five if you count the SP?

Anyway this news is great.

Here's what ConnectWise's head honcho Arnie Bellini said about the

Xerox/Connectwise API swap (Tip: To impersonate Arnie, read it as fast as you possibly can, without passing out)

"Solution providers must excel at providing MPS if they want to keep pace with forecasted demand. Our new integration with Xerox will help ConnectWise partners deliver these services at attractive price points for the end user while giving solution providers a recurring revenue stream for a service that's nearly effortless to deploy."

I once affectionately called Arnie Bellini a flamboyant leader. He doesn't invite me to speak at his Tampa shindigs anymore.

Contemplate This, Then Monetize It

I didn't know that 38 percent of U.S. travelers will pay more to travel companies that protect the environment.

But I am damn glad to hear that 61 percent of them said they would pay up to 10 percent more.

These numbers from the Travel Industry of America tell me there's gold beneath the grass of this here green movement. And the great thing about selling with a green angle is that it drips with irresistible sales and marketing aphrodisiac. Being green is a concern for the customer, it's a concern for the community, it's a way to save money, it's a way to save energy, it's a way to reduce waste, you get just as much performance, greenhouses gases are reduced, customers respect it, great vendors practice it and it's a way to give all the children on
Earth a brighter future.

You get the idea.

So this rant (and its associated research) began after I noticed the Energy Star seal on the side of my new Xerox WorkCentre 3210 and decided to figure out just what it meant.

Turns out Energy Star was born in 1992 when the EPA and the DoE launched a voluntary labeling program to promote energy-efficient products that reduce greenhouse gas emissions. Computers and monitors were the first products to get the Energy Star label, by the way.

The Energy Star folks tell us that if a typical household spends $2,000 a year on energy bills, a fleet of Energy Star devices substituted in would save them 30 percent, or more than 700 bucks a year, with no sacrifice in performance.

And if all computers sold in the U.S. were Energy Star-certified, we'd save $2 billion a year and reduce greenhouse gas emissions equal to the amount of emissions released by 2 million cars.

# Remember the Lesson of Nick Overall!

Nick Overall, a high school friend I finally met again last week after too many years, is an architect in Norwalk, N.J. Nick was just named "Tree Advocate of the Year" by the Norwalk city fathers just 'cause

Nick doesn't mow down a lot of trees by default when he creates a building. Nick got his picture in the paper, a nice little ceremony, the whole nine yards, and now he can market his business behind the award and drive new revenues, at a premium no less, when he can! (cue flashback music)

Thirty-eight percent of U.S. travelers will pay more to travel companies that protect the environment.

I'll tell you how you can get your customers profitable green recognition in their communities in my next blog.

Sorry, my editors want me to keep these short. Jerks.

Can We Get Back to This Now?

When we last left our subject of monetizing the green movement, I was saying my editors were jerks.

They have corrected me.

Now ... The question was: How can your customers get "green recognition" in their communities that they can use in their marketing campaigns and messaging to drive more business? (If you're totally lost, read my last blog, the section about "The Lesson of Nick Overall" where all the scary music comes in.)

Send the customer to "The Portfolio Manager" on the Energy Star site.

(If you are lost, I bet this at least sounds really cool, huh?)

There, they can start to use Portfolio Manager, a nifty, interactive energy management tool that will track and assess their energy and water consumption, all in a secure online environment that won't freak them out privacy-wise.

Then, once they've upgraded their printers and IT infrastructures to include more Energy Star machines, and adopted your powermanagement recommendations and deployed other upgrades you advised, they can use Portfolio Manager to share data with the EPA and get EPA recognition!

Literally, they have award levels your customers can take to the bank.

Energy Star label -- Superior energy performance in a single building.

Energy Star Leaders -- Organizationwide energy performance

Energy Star Partner of the Year -- Outstanding contributions to reducing greenhouse gas emissions through energy efficiency

I'm telling ya, a dry cleaner chain or a private sanitation company or a check-processing company (with a green "direct deposit" spin) or an architect firm can each hang a shingle outside their businesses harping an Energy Star accolade, and more business will come in than before.

But I know you. Right now you're quietly asking, "Well that's all great Paige, but how the heck do you think we're going to get these customers to upgrade their IT infrastructures to include more Energy Star machines, and adopt our power-management recommendations and deploy other upgrades that of course we've have been recommending they freakin' buy?!"

Excellent question.

Tell customers all the new green gear is a major tax deduction. Which it is, thanks to President Obama, who extended the Depreciation and

Section 179 Expense until the end of this year.

Here's how it works:

• Customers make a technology investment in 2009
• They calculate its depreciation at this IRS site
• They deduct up to $250,000 on their 2009 taxes
• The tax breaks are up to 50 percent of the cost of the new stuff!

Example: Computers are a five-year property, according to the IRS. A customer who purchases $20,000 in computer systems can deduct $2,304, plus an extra 50 percent depreciation allowance, for off-the shelf computer software.

Isn't this fun?

## How I'll Remember This Week--Part I

Boy, they sure suddenly got all mean over there at The Databazaar
Blog.

The blog is collared to the print and imaging reseller site Databazaar.com, but the blog's writers this week sound a tad hostile.

Well, maybe not hostile, but filled with that same passive-aggressive kind of nonsense you hear when a flaky help-desk tech begins coloring his customer-service repertoire with constant subreferences to how technology will ultimately destroy humanity.

"If the Lexmark T652n and the Lexmark T654n were role-playing characters, they'd belong to the Thief class," one blog entry reads.

"We suspect HP is more concerned about supplies than printers because that's where the big money lies," another reads from the day before.

OK. So it's not that these blog entries are a pack of screaming lies. But even I get squeamish when I read product smack-downs sponsored by a "value-added-reseller" doing its darnedest to hock the very same equipment.

Oh, look away, look away...

How I'll Remember This Week--Part II

Wow. Now this is much better.

Having deployed a nice set of Xerox 980s, which are hot-shot continuous-feed (900 ppm!!) commercial color printers (boy, how I'd love one in my living room!), the nice chaps at London's MBA Group got a visit from Xerox's president and incoming chief executive Ursula
Burns.

Burns dropped by "after hearing about the level of colour reproduction being achieved on the presses."
MBA chairman Bachar Aintaoui said the installation of the Xerox equipment was completed so efficiently "due to the efforts of MBA staff and the Xerox engineers."

He added: "It's great that our skill in colour reproduction is also being acknowledged and we were honored to meet the president of
Xerox."

This, my friends, is how you spread the love.
Mass Production Books Are Now Rare and Nostalgic--Let's Make Some Money

It's easy to read a news story like this and get all choked up from a romanticism with the publishing industry:

"As the publishing industry continues to fragment, many of its best growth opportunities are in small places, with profits realized from efficient, low-cost processes."

These views by publishing consultant Lauren Dawson during Xerox's recent Thought Leadership Workshop on digital books were followed by some pretty clear trend factoids we've each noticed: Fewer big printings of mass-market titles and more short-run and on-demand printings available for smaller fan bases. Seems that's just the way art forms evolve. Discovery of the classics takes place at the population level, then the population fragments into a much larger number of more specific tastes.

Between late 1964 and 1966 the Billboard Top 100 was constantly filled with songs by only three groups: The Stones, The Beatles and
Bob Dylan.

This is unthinkable today. The listener base is so fragmented into individual tastes, and the technology--having moved from vinyl to
CD to MP-whatever--has commoditized to the point where short run is affordable.

Today, your album may be selling more copies than anyone else's, but there are a lot more "else's" out there, so record sales no longer ensure a political or style constituency.

Meaning ... There's opportunity in this fragmentation, which Dawson notes as she points out that most of the publishing industry's projected growth "is either in 'power hits' (think Harry Potter) produced the traditional way, or in alternatives offered by in-store printing, self-publishing, regional and small presses, as well as digital print–on-demand."

"A key enabler is digital print-on-demand, which will grow significantly as it continues to boost efficiency in the supply chain."

Thanks, Lauren. We're on your side.

## Let It Bleed

I've told you before that I'm an ink-stained wretch and proud of it.

Which is why this spectacular quote from Steve Reynolds, an analyst with Lyra Research, which follows the printing and imaging industries, strikes such a chord with me.

Asked what he thinks about new Xerox President Ursula M. Burns, who's taking over for the retiring Anne Mulcahy, Reynolds tells us:

"They're both insiders that sort of bleed toner, as it were."

Trend Abuse Alert — Beware: "ADFs As Next Wave"

You know by now I'm a skeptic.

But I do at least follow my fact-ridden bashings with some fresh alternative ideas, right? ... Anyone?

So, I see this headline on cartridgenews.com that sez: EMERGING

TRENDS: Auto Document Feeders in Multifunction Printers

Here's their point:

"One feature we see more and more in multifunction printers is the office-friendly auto-document feeder, or ADF. This special tray is designed to simplify an all-in-one printer's non-printing functions such as copying, scanning and faxing."

I'm not sure what happened next. After reading this story, I got up, walked outside, had a smoke, then came back in and sat down. This was on my screen when I awoke:

"ADFs were designed to keep office workers from having to copy multiple-hundred-page manuscripts one page at a time. They behave poorly with any stock other than 20-60-pound bond and copy paper, so whatever this new trend story is talking about as far as ADFs being the answer to not having to put photo paper in a tray (dedicated or not) is very much like that rock band from outer space that appeared on the "Flintstones:" The Way Outs. ("We're goin' Way out! Way Out!")"

Go ahead. Slide a stack of photo paper in your nearest ADF. See those little lines running across the surface of your freshly drying color print? They're called roller marks. (Hint: Photo paper best feeds flat, not coming off a 180-degree curl.)

The idea that ADFs solve the multiple paper tray problem is also a little murky here. Your fax and your printed e-mail are all going to be on the same paper (unless you want to crack the tray open and load in some goldenrod).

But OK, rather than bash, I'll give my own vision of where this all is headed.

ADFs will not be the next wave of anything, but instead will fade.

This is why: There are only two kinds of print jobs. The one you care about, and the one you don't. There is no in between. And just because you don't care about it doesn't mean you don't need it. Think "homework."

The MFP technology most offices need right now has to accommodate some increasingly arcane data-transfer methods like (yes, everyone hold hands) faxing, and (squeeze tighter) scanning.

See, we said it. It's OK.

Did I forget copying? That will be done with a pen-sized device you wand over a page in less than five years.

Faxing and scanning each assume the document was not created or modified (signed, stamped, etc.) on a computer.

"Can't I just email it, why do I have to fax it? You can't just send me the file? Why do you have to scan it?"

These two questions are ending the lives of faxing and scanning in the workplace. If you ask me, they're already dead. The body just hasn't hit the floor yet.

Typical office MFP systems of the near future (which will not be called that, look for something more markety) will have a single print path to ensure calibration and no paper tray, just a single feeder that accepts any type stock, or envelope, making it the responsibility of the employee to take as much paper to the printer as he or she thinks is needed (there's your green reminder).

Take-away: Beware journalists hawking trends.

# We Just Wasted All the Money in the U.S.A!

I'm absolutely certain—though still not so sure—what the so-called sponsors of this report were given as motivation for its creation, assuming they knew what the outcome of their report would be: A mindless and unmanaged crack-down on government printing, executed by, and under the quality control of, the very same folks the report claims can't temper their urge to hit the print command habitually.

The report's slide preso, posted on Govexec.com, informs us simple folk that:

• The federal government spends nearly $1.3 billion annually on employee printing.

• Of these costs, the federal government spends $440.4 million each year on unnecessary printing.

Yes, $440.4 million is a hair-curling figure when imagined as money going down the drain.

But there's more. Here's my favorite factoid in the deck:

• The federal government spends $440.4 million per year on unnecessary printing, more than $1 million per day—almost as much as it costs to print actual currency. Get it? The U.S. spends $492.8

million a year to print up all our paper money, and in that same year it'll waste $440.4 million printing something for nothing.

(Editor's note: Paige has requested she have editorial leeway to say the following, which are solely her views. "Before we all feel sorry for the U.S. wasting almost the same amount of money it takes to make all the paper money we have, let's be reminded that the U.S. "makes money" making money, too. It's called seigniorage, which is the margin between the cost of producing a coin and its currency value.

And it works with paper money too when hoarded old bills get taxed as they re-enter the financial system after newly designed bills begin circulation."—End Editor's note—)

Anyway, before we get all crazy here and I get blamed for being wasteful-minded and not thinking green for making fun of an idea to cut unnecessary printing, what the government needs is a practical managed print system that makes print costs not just negligible when balanced against ROI, but also a more important part of a successful business equation.

Besides, if government employees have been print, print, printing away, it's because printing helps drive productivity (for gosh sakes it's on slide 7 of their own preso)

## "Our Love Is in A Time Capsule"

Here's a little story for ya.

When I was a young buck reporter for InfoWorld Magazine in San

Francisco way back in 1999, I was given a demo of a new, widely available Xerox solid ink color printer that literally knocked me off my freakin' heels.

Here was the future, I thought. Solid ink with no wasteful, disposable toner-casing, that melts images on a print drum blanket in much the same way a 4-color, 32-inch Heidelberg reprints classic works of art sold as high-dollar prints.(Yes, I threw paper behind a 32-inch Heidy to get through college.

Nightshift. You're called "the feeder", and you basically run the press while the printer calibrates, dampens rollers, yells at his wife over the phone, and pulls sheets he loupes to examine the CMYK Rosetta pattern of the four plates. Cool stuff. You know already…)

Anyway, so a week or so ago along comes New York Times technology reporter Ashlee Vance (a fellow colleague of mine at that Infoworld estate of old) with this report, which truly sunk my heart.

It's absence of history was shocking.

Writes Vance:

"After years of research, Xerox will release the first in a new series of large machines this month that it claims will change the economics of printing large volumes of color documents at offices. Unlike traditional laser printers that use cartridges of powdery, sometimes messy toner, the revamped products rely on hunks of ink that remain solid at room temperature and then melt when heated."

I'm sorry. Did I just dream about seeing that freaking super cool
Xerox solid ink color printer working and for sale back in 1999? I was in San Francisco back then, right?

Ashlee even describes it just like I saw it, whatever I thought it was:

"And instead of putting clunky cartridges of toner into the printers, customers just pop in the sticks of ink. Once that ink runs out, another stick goes in, and there's nothing that needs to be thrown away or recycled."

OK, so the only crime committed by my friend Ashlee Vance is using the term "new" to describe something that has been a country mile ahead of conventional print thinking for almost two decades. This from Xerox's own FAQ page on solid ink (which Ashlee could have
Googled, no? Huh?)

"Xerox announced it's first solid ink printer in 1991, and its groundbreaking capabilities immediately won Editors' Choice Awards from PC Magazine, MacUser, and MacWorld. Successive solid ink products have won over 50 major awards. Now more than ever, businesses, schools, and other organizations are taking advantage of solid ink's unique color quality, speed, reliability, ease of use, and low cost."

Guess I shouldn't be so hard on Ashlee. Other old colleagues of mine gave the story the same treatment.

# Potty Time

Our Question of the Week this week dared to ask which one word best describes 2009?

You did not shy away.

The non-scientific straw poll went to the glass-half-full consortium.

About 70 percent responded with a positive term.

We had one flip-flopper, two rule-breakers, only one ALL CAP

WRITER, and to my surprise, those of you who chose to cast your entry under the anonymous protection of the Business Transformation Site tempered your responses quite prudishly. About as bad as it got in there was a reference to using the toilet.

Some notables: Payback, lame, enlightening, BS, and my favorite one (no, we did not stuff the ballot): Transformation.

This Kinda Stuff Just Makes Me Plain Crazy

A story about a shady contractor stealing and selling on eBay boxes of XEROX solid ink sticks and cartridges to the tune of $150,000.

"Quick service, good product at a good price," one eBay buyer raved about this guy's service.

"Very fast shipping, excellent communications," another wrote. "A fine chap."

Man, I hate seeing a great customer service professional end up on the wrong side of the law.

But boy does this legitimize the fact that there exists a huge market out there for excess toner, which you might be buying for your print customers!

# Inside Larry Ellison's House

The last time I was at Larry Ellison's house he had some tech guys working out the bugs of his indoor Japanese boat ride.

The Oracle boss built an internal river that runs through the Atherton, Calif., mansion he's still erecting in the woods outside Silicon Valley.

With the touch of a handheld remote, a small Japanese-style boat (or a convoy of them, if you hit the blue button) floats into the room and allows you to step in for a slow ride through Larry's Japan-laden digs over water calm enough to sip sake upon.

The problem with the boat ride had to do with the fog machine. One of the buttons on the remote feeds a misty dry-ice fog over the shallow indigo river. But for some reason, this feature simply wasn't operating the last time I was there.

This did not please Larry, who was already having a bad day. Deer sensors around the Atherton compound were suddenly sending a flurry of false positives, confusing the security system, which protested just as conversations peaked.

He kept his chin up, but I do remember feeling sort of sorry for Larry that day.

Now, the first time I told a friend I felt sorry for Larry Ellison, she looked at me like a person who'd just heard a dog speak perfect English for 15 seconds. But the feeling did come over me, which is why I smiled reading the January 2010 issue of Wired magazine last weekend, and its salute to Larry's vision of the thin client, as opposed to Bill Gates' fat client. (2010 issue? Subscribers get pubs early.)

In the issue, Wired editors give Larry his due for envisioning cloud computing years ahead of time as the Network Computer, which never got a business footing, but was spot-on when it came to the direction client computing has always been headed: Intelligence in the cloud as a utility; simple interface with no innards at your fingertips.

The Wired article is a great story and also addresses the often-omitted history of how Larry was repeatedly doomed to play second fiddle to Gates' PR successes, all while possessing and preaching a sounder technology vision than the Microsoft magnate.

There's a soul-lifting lesson too.

As we say farewell to 2009, let us remember that in technology, the vision that scales is the vision that survives. Such vision requires a serious recognition and acceptance of your surroundings, and a selfless acknowledgement that others will indeed move ahead of you at times, before your vision prevails. Think: Tucker, the car maker. Or the neutral, convenience-computing vision of the Xerox Alto PC prototype. Or networked storage.

I was standing next to Bill Gates backstage in Las Vegas after his 1999 Comdex keynote, and as we chatted, I mentioned that the owner of

Mall.com told me he thought Gates' vision was too conservative. Gates bristled. "Compared to what?" he demanded.

See what I mean?

Can I Xerox That for You?

Published by Electric Loser Land
51 Sixth Street, San Francisco, California 94103
*ELL* 2018
Copyright 2011 United Business Media, Manhasset, New York
ISBN **13:** 978-1508909514

~

www.ingramcontent.com/pod-product-compliance
Lightning Source LLC
Chambersburg PA
CBHW060951050326
40689CB00012B/2631